# ATHENS

teNeues

# ATHENS

**Photographs by Vassilis Gonis / PhoZ**
**Text by Dimitris Angelis**

**teNeues**

When, in 1897—a year after the first modern Olympic Games—the American diplomat George Horton wrote about Athens 'of dust and of violet sunsets', the Greek capital was still more like a large village and not the broad cosmopolitan city that visitors are facing, with surprise, nowadays. Even so, certain of its features remain unaltered through time, despite its gigantic enlargement due to urbanism and an attack of the bulimic force of cement: one year before 2004, Athens remains drowned in that same dust, due to the intense preparations for the upcoming Olympics. From the old port of Pireas and the beach of Faliro, all the way to Marathon, crews of thousands of workers operate restlessly day and night, deafening sounds of excavations echo endlessly, and a sneaky cloud of dust crawls all over them, sliding through the narrowest cracks, sticking to the skin, so that eventually it is impossible to breathe.

But still, when the feverish force of the noisy crowd ceases and the intense working rhythmus loosen, the sunsets in this dusty city are equally as violet and dreamy as they used to be... Athens lives mostly at night. For at that time, under the landscape, wounded by the constructions, overshadowed by the "crazy" mount of Imittos and brightened by the holy rock of Acropolis, the eternal grace and the magic of this place is revealed—and along with it, the hospitality and the open-heartedness of its people. It is this tempting, deeply humane, intensely erotic night, filled with anticipation when anything seems possible, that truly makes Athens unique amongst other European capitals.

All the same, the Greek capital remains a mosaic city. And I do not simply say that with respect to the monuments that interact upon these glorious grounds: the combination of ancient, Roman, Byzantine, Muslim, early twentieth-century neoclassical and modern constructions, composes a thick text, made up by consequent layers of scriptures, left behind by the residents of this eternal city; I also speak of the contradictory sentiments inscribed on the heart of a most sensitive visitor: uneven emotions ranging from irritation and fury to worshipful admiration and longing. For, contemporary Athens remains essentially a noncompliant city, trying obstinately, and sometimes clumsily or even childishly, to enchant you. It mobilizes its glorious past, proclaims its European character proudly and opens up its eastern heart magnanimously. And you, slightly lost within all this, finally give in to its temptations without a trace of resistance, possibly because you know that it is constantly growing and changing and perhaps it will soon not be the same anymore.

*Dimitris Angelis*

Als 1897 – also ein Jahr nach den ersten modernen Olympischen Spielen – der amerikanische Diplomat George Horton Athen beschrieb, als „aus Staub und violetten Sonnenuntergängen" bestehend, war die griechische Hauptstadt noch eher ein großes Dorf als die ausgedehnte Weltstadt, die Besucher heute mit Erstaunen ansehen. Und dennoch hat manches Charakteristische die Zeiten überdauert, ungeachtet des gigantischen Wachstums als Folge von Landflucht und einer geradezu eruptiven Ausschüttung von Beton: Ein Jahr vor 2004 versinkt Athen durch die Vorbereitungen zu den Olympischen Spielen im selben Staub. Vom alten Hafen von Piräus und dem Strand von Faliro bis nach Marathon arbeiten Trupps von tausenden von Arbeitern ohne Unterbrechung Tag und Nacht, der ohrenbetäubende Lärm der Grabungen dröhnt pausenlos und über allem kriecht leise eine Staubwolke, die durch die schmalsten Ritzen dringt und sich auf der Haut niederschlägt, sodass es manchmal unmöglich ist, Luft zu bekommen.

Doch die Sonnenuntergänge in dieser staubigen Stadt sind genauso violett und verträumt wie eh und je, wenn das fiebrige Gedränge der lärmenden Menschenmassen weniger wird und sich der intensive Rhythmus der Arbeit verliert … Athen lebt vor allem bei Nacht. Denn zu dieser Zeit, in dieser Landschaft, die verwundet ist durch Baustellen, überschattet vom „verrückten" Berg Imittos und erhellt durch den heiligen Felsen der Akropolis, zeigen sich die immerwährende Anmut und der Zauber dieses Ortes – und zugleich die Gastfreundschaft und die Herzlichkeit seiner Bewohner. Es ist diese bewegende, zutiefst menschliche, intensiv erotische Nacht, angefüllt mit Erwartung, denn alles scheint möglich zu sein, die Athen einzigartig macht unter den Hauptstädten Europas.

Zugleich ist und bleibt die griechische Hauptstadt ein urbanes Mosaik. Ich sage das nicht einfach nur im Hinblick auf die Baudenkmäler, die auf diesem berühmten Boden miteinander in Beziehung stehen: die Verbindung des Antiken, Römischen, Byzantinischen, Muslimischen und des Historismus am Beginn des zwanzigsten Jahrhunderts mit den modernen Bauten ergibt einen dicht komponierten Text, der aus der Folge übereinandergelagerter Schriften besteht, die von den Bewohnern dieser ewigen Stadt hinterlassen wurden. Ich spreche auch von den widersprüchlichen Gefühlen, eingeschrieben in das Herz eines überaus sensitiven Besuchers: unterschiedliche Emotionen in einer Bandbreite von Irritation und Panik bis zu verehrender Bewunderung und Sehnsucht. Denn das heutige Athen ist im Grunde seines Wesens eine widerspenstige Stadt, die hartnäckig und manchmal auf eine unbeholfene oder gar kindische Art und Weise versucht, zu bezaubern. Athen hält die Vergangenheit lebendig, proklamiert stolz seinen europäischen Charakter und öffnet großmütig sein orientalisches Herz. Und du, ein bisschen verloren zwischen alledem, gibst dich schließlich seinen Versuchungen hin, ohne eine Spur des Widerstands, vielleicht weil du weißt, dass es stetig wächst und sich verändert und dass es möglicherweise bald ganz anders sein wird.

*Dimitris Angelis*

Lorsqu'en 1897, c'est-à-dire un an après les premiers Jeux olympiques modernes, le diplomate américain Georges Horton écrivait sur Athènes « de la poussière et des couchers de soleil violets », la capitale de la Grèce n'était qu'un gros village et pas la grande ville cosmopolite que le visiteur contemple aujourd'hui avec étonnement. Et pourtant, certains traits n'ont pas été altérés par le temps, malgré son agrandissement à la suite de l'exode rural et des assauts boulimiques du béton : un an avant 2004, Athènes étouffe toujours dans la poussière à cause des préparations intensives des Jeux olympiques. De l'ancien port du Pirée et de la baie de Faliro jusqu'à Marathon, des milliers d'ouvriers travaillent jour et nuit, dans un bruit assourdissant, sous un nuage de poussière qui s'infiltre dans le moindre interstice, colle à la peau et rend l'air presque irrespirable.

Mais quand l'effervescence des masses bruyantes retombe et que les rythmes intensifs de travail se relâchent, les couchers de soleil sur cette ville poussiéreuse redeviennent violets et font rêver comme avant … Athènes vit surtout la nuit. Parce que c'est le moment où réapparaissent, sous le paysage blessé par l'urbanisme, dans l'ombre de la « folle » montagne Hymette et dans la lumière du rocher sacré de l'Acropole, le charme éternel et la magie de ce lieu – ainsi que l'hospitalité et le grand cœur de ses habitants. Ces nuits émouvantes, profondément humaines et intensément érotiques, marquées par l'attente, quand tout semble possible, fait d'Athènes une ville unique comparée aux autres capitales européennes.

En même temps, la capitale grecque est et demeure une mosaïque. Je ne dis pas seulement cela à cause de tous les monuments qui ont été construits sur cette illustre terre : les différentes architectures, antique, romaine, byzantine, musulmane, néoclassique du début du XXe siècle et moderne, forment un vaste ensemble de strates tel un texte écrit successivement par les habitants de cette ville éternelle. Je parle aussi des sentiments contradictoires qu'elle inspire à des visiteurs très sensibles : une multitude de sentiments qui oscillent entre irritation et fureur, adoration et nostalgie. Car l'Athènes contemporaine reste, au fond, une ville insoumise qui essaie obstinément, d'une manière souvent maladroite ou même puérile, de fasciner. Elle mobilise son passé glorieux, proclame avec fierté son caractère européen et ouvre généreusement son cœur d'orientale. Et toi, un peu perdu dans tout cela, tu finis par céder à ses attraits sans l'ombre d'une résistance, peut-être parce que tu sais qu'elle ne cesse de se développer et de changer et qu'elle ne sera sans doute plus la même bientôt.

*Dimitris Angelis*

Cuando en 1897, es decir, un año después de los primeros Juegos Olímpicos modernos, el diplomático americano George Horton escribió sobre la Atenas "del polvo y de los crepúsculos violetas", la capital de Grecia aún era, desde luego, una gran aldea y no la amplia ciudad cosmopolita que con sorpresa contempla el visitante actual. Y aún así, determinadas características permanecen en ella inalteradas a lo largo del tiempo, pese al engrandecimiento impuesto por el éxodo rural y el movimiento bulímico del cemento: un año antes del 2004, Atenas permanece ahogada en aquel mismo polvo a causa de las obras para la preparación de los próximos Juegos Olímpicos. Desde el antiguo puerto de El Pireo y la playa de Fáliro hasta Maratón, talleres de miles de obreros trabajan día y noche sin descanso, un ruido ensordecedor se oye por todas partes y, por encima de todo, se arrastra una nube astuta de polvo que atraviesa las grietas más cerradas, pegándose a la piel de forma que al final no puedes respirar.

Pero los crepúsculos de esta polvorienta ciudad, cuando se apacigua el movimiento febril del mundo bullicioso y se relajan los ritmos intensos del trabajo, se muestran de nuevo igual de violeta y ensoñadores que entonces... Atenas vive sobre todo de noche. Porque a aquella hora, bajo el paisaje herido por las construcciones que la alocada montaña conocida como Himeto ensombrece y que la roca sagrada de la Acrópolis ilumina, sólo se distinguen la gracia eterna y la magia del lugar a la vez que el carácter hospitalario y de gran corazón de sus habitantes. Esta noche seductora y profundamente humana, intensamente erótica, llena de expectación ya que en ella todo se presenta de repente como posible, hace a Atenas verdaderamente única entre las otras grandes ciudades de Europa.

Por lo demás, la capital de Grecia permanece como una ciudad mosaica. Y no me refiero sólo a causa de los monumentos que revisten su gloriosa tierra: antiguos, romanos, bizantinos, de la dominación turca, neoclásicos de principios del siglo pasado; todos juntos componen un texto denso por los sucesivos revestimientos de los escritos que dejaron tras ellos los habitantes de esta ciudad eterna. Hablo al mismo tiempo de los sentimientos refutados que graba en su corazón su visitante más sensible, sentimientos insólitos que fluctúan desde la ira y la crispación hasta la admiración piadosa y la ensoñación. Puesto que la Atenas contemporánea permanece, en el fondo, como una ciudad insumisa que intenta de manera obstinada, frecuentemente con torpeza o incluso de manera infantil, fascinarte. Moviliza su pasado glorioso, proclama a voces su carácter europeo, te abre generosamente su corazón oriental. Y tú, perdido en medio de todo esto, te entregas finalmente a sus encantos sin oponer la menor resistencia, tal vez porque sabes que ella crece siempre y cambia y que tal vez en poco tiempo ya no sea la misma.

*Dimitris Angelis*

Allorché nel 1897, un anno dopo le prime Olimpiadi dell'era moderna, il diplomatico statunitense George Horton descrisse Atene come "fatta di polvere e tramonti viola", la città era ancora piuttosto un grande villaggio, e non la grande città cosmopolita che si trovano di fronte, sorpresi, i viaggiatori dei giorni nostri. E tuttavia alcune caratteristiche sono sopravvissute, nonostante la gigantesca crescita conseguente alla fuga dalle campagne e all'attacco bulimico del cemento: un anno prima del 2004, a causa dei preparativi per le Olimpiadi, Atene sprofonda nella stessa polvere di allora. Dall'antico porto del Pireo e dalla spiaggia di Faliro fino a Maratona squadre di migliaia di operai lavorano senza pause, giorno e notte, il rumore assordante degli scavi echeggia incessantemente e sopra a tutto si stende silenziosa una nuvola di polvere che penetra fin nelle minime fessure e va a posarsi sulla pelle, tanto che a volte non si riesce a respirare.

Ma, quando la ressa febbrile della folla rumorosa si placa e il ritmo intenso del lavoro si perde, i tramonti in questa polverosa città sono ancora viola e languidi come un tempo ... Atene vive soprattutto di notte: allora in questo panorama ferito dai cantieri, sovrastato dal "folle" monte Imetto e schiarito dal sacro colle dell'Acropoli, si rivelano l'eterna grazia e la magia di questo posto, ed al contempo l'ospitalità e la cordialità dei suoi abitanti. È questa notte allettante, profondamente umana, intensamente erotica, piena di aspettative perché tutto pare possibile, a rendere Atene unica fra le capitali europee.

Al tempo stesso la capitale greca rimane un mosaico urbano. Non lo dico solo per quanto riguarda i monumenti che "interagiscono" su questa celebre terra: dalla combinazione degli edifici greco antichi, romani, bizantini, musulmani, neoclassici d'inizio Novecento e moderni risulta un testo denso, composto dal susseguirsi di documenti lasciati, strato dopo strato, dagli abitanti di questa città eterna. Intendo parlare anche dei sentimenti contrastanti, incisi nel cuore di un visitatore oltremodo sensibile: le più disparate emozioni, dall'irritazione all'ira, alla rispettosa ammirazione e alla bramosia. Perché l'Atene di oggi è essenzialmente una città non remissiva, che testardamente e a volte in maniera goffa o persino infantile cerca di ammaliare. Atene mantiene vivo il passato, proclama con orgoglio il suo carattere europeo ed apre magnanima il proprio cuore orientale. E tu, un po' smarrito fra tutto ciò, ti abbandoni alla fine alle sue tentazioni, senza opporre resistenza, forse perché sai che cresce e si trasforma in continuazione e che probabilmente presto sarà completamente diversa.

*Dimitris Angelis*

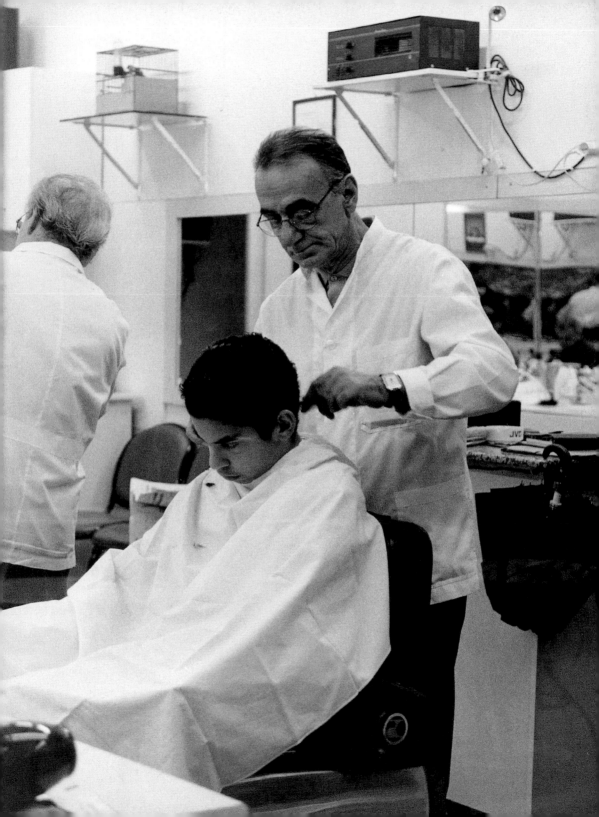

# Directory    Verzeichnis    Table des matières    Directorio    Indice delle materie

2      Acropolis and Pireas seen from Likavittos Hill

4      Statue of Athena in front of the Academy of Athens

10/11  Acropolis and Pireas seen from Likavittos Hill

12     Monastiraki Square

13     Ermou Street

14     Ermou Street

15     Ermou Street, Man with Laterna

16     Ermou Street

17     Ermou Street

18     Ermou Street, Kapnikarea Church

       At the Corner of Eolou and Agias Irinis Street

19     Eolou Street

20     Psiri District

21     Psiri District

22     Euripidou Street

23     Psiri District

       Euripidou Street

24     Psiri District, Lepeniotou Street

25     Psiri District, Miaouli Street

26     Psiri District, Easter Market, Naxos Island Producers

27     Psiri District, Easter Market, Naxos Island Producers

28     Monastiraki Market, Avissinias Square

       Monastirkai Market, Ifestou Street

29     Monastirkai Market, People Playing Tavli

       Monastirkai Market, Ifestou Street

30     Theseion, Temple of Hephaestus

31     Stoa of Attalos, Museum

32     Ancient Agora

       Aerides District, Roman Agora

33     Aerides District, Andronikos Kyrrhestes Clock, Tower of the Winds

34     Aerides District

35     Aerides District, Markou Avriliou Street

       Dionisiou Areopagitou Street

36     Aerides District, Roman Agora

37     Aerides District

38     Aerides District

39     Aerides District

40     Panormou Avenue, Traditional Tavern

41     Neapoli District, Traditional Tavern

42     Dionisiou Areopagitou Street, Agia Sofia Church

43     Dionisiou Areopagitou Street, Agia Sofia Church

44     Tritis Septemvriou Street

45     At the Corner of Panepistimiou and Eolou Street

46     Vassileos Konstantinou Avenue

47     Neapoli District

48     Koukaki District

49     Acropolis Metro Station

50/51  Acropolis and Herodes Atticus Odeon seen from Philopappous Hill

52     Acropolis, Propylaen

53     Acropolis, Erechtheion

54     Monument on Top of Philopappous Hill

55     Herodes Atticus Odeon and Philopappous Hill

56     Zappeion

57     Zappeion

58     Greek Parliament Building, Monument of the Unknown Soldier

59     Greek Parliament Building, Monument of the Unknown Soldier

60     At the Corner of Vassileos Georgiou A' Street and Panepistimiou Street, Hotel Grande Bretagne

61     Stadiou Street, National Historical Museum and Statue of Kolokotronis

62     Arsakion Megaro, Stadiou Street

63     Stadiou Street

64     Stoa Orfeos, Café

       Stadiou Street

65     Stoa Orfeos

66     Neapoli Dirstrict, Pantopolion (Corner Shop)

       Voukourestiou Street, Café

| | |
|---|---|
| 67 | Near Syntagma Square, Barber's Shop |
| 68 | Corner of Kanari Street and Solonos Street |
| | Solonos Street, Shop Selling Bugatses |
| 69 | Agii Theodori Square, Agii Theodori Church |
| 70 | Korai Street |
| 71 | At the Corner of Panepistimiou and Riga Fereou Street |
| 72 | Omonia Square, Kiosk |
| 73 | Panepistimiou Street near Omonia Square |
| | Panepistimiou Street, Coulouria and Loucoumades Seller |
| 74 | Athinas Street, Town Hall, Statue of Periclis |
| 75 | Panepistimiou Street, National Library |
| 76 | Panepistimiou Street, Academy of Athens |
| 77 | Panepistimiou Street, Academy of Athens, Statue of Apollo |
| 78 | Panepistimiou Street, Schliemann's House, Numismatic Museum |
| 79 | Panepistimiou Street, Schliemann's House, Numismatic Museum |
| 80 | At the Corner of Akadimias Street and Ippokratous Street |
| | Akadimias Street, Zoodohos Pigi Church |
| 81 | Akadimias Street, Bus Station |
| 82 | Vassileos Konstantinou Avenue, Likavittos Hill |
| | Vassilisis Sofias Avenue, The Glass Runner |
| 83 | Ampelokipi District, Vassilisis Sofias Avenue, Tower of Athens |
| | Vassilisis Sofias Avenue, Megaro Musikis |
| 84 | Vassilisis Sofias Avenue, Museum of Cycladic Art |
| 85 | Vassilisis Sofias Avenue, Byzantine and Christian Museum |
| 86 | Petraki Monastery |
| 87 | Petraki Monastery |
| 88 | Likavittos Hill over the Rooftops of Anafiotika District |
| 89 | Likavittos Hill, Agios Georgios Chapel |
| 90 | Exharhia District, Kallidromiou Street, Market |
| 91 | Exharhia District, Kallidromiou Street, Market |
| 92 | Exharhia District, Café |
| 93 | Alexandras Avenue, Pedion Areos Park |
| | Alexandras Avenue, Panathinea Park, Chess and Card Players |
| 94 | Omonia Square |
| 95 | Omonia Square |
| | Omonia Square |
| 96 | Agiou Konstantinou Avenue, National Theater |
| 97 | Patision Avenue, National Archeological Museum |
| 98 | Patision Avenue |
| 99 | Patision Avenue |
| 100 | Patision Avenue |
| 101 | Patision Avenue |
| | Café in the Cultural Center of Athens Municipal |
| 102 | Parade at 28th of October (Panepistimiou Street) |
| 103 | Parade at 28th of October (Panepistimiou Street) |
| 104 | Parade at 25th of March (Panepistimiou Street) |
| 105 | Parade at 25th of March (Panepistimiou Street) |
| 106 | Arahovis Street, Easter Friday |
| 107 | Nea Makri, Easter Service |
| 108 | Asklipiou Street, Agios Nikolaos Pefkakion Church, Easter Friday |
| 109 | Asklipiou Street, Agios Nikolaos Pefkakion Church, Easter Friday |
| 110 | Agios Ioannis Rendi District, Village Cinemas |
| 111 | Agios Ioannis Rendi District, Allou Fun Park |
| 112 | Nea Ionia District, Athens 2004 Olympic Committee Main Facilities |
| | Nikea District, Weight Lifting Center |
| 113 | Nikea District, Weight Lifting Center |
| 114 | Markopoulo, Ippodromos of Athens |
| 115 | Markopoulo, Olympic Equestrian Stadium |
| 116 | Pireas |
| 117 | Pireas Port |

Front cover: Acropolis and Pireas seen from
          Likavittos Hill
Back cover: Monastiraki Square

Photographs © 2004 Vassilis Gonis
© 2004 teNeues Verlag GmbH + Co. KG, Kempen
All rights reserved.

Vassilis Gonis
Haralampi 4
11472 Neapoli, Athens
Greece

vgonis2002@yahoo.com

Photographs by Vassilis Gonis / PhoZ
Design by Anika Leppkes
Introduction by Dimitris Angelis, Athens
English translation by Christina Georgiou, Athens
Translation by SWB Communications,
Dr. Sabine Werner-Birkenbach, Mainz
Dr. Sabine Werner-Birkenbach (German)
Dominique Le Pluart (French)
Virgínia López Recio (Spanish)
Dr. Nicoletta Negri (Italian)
Editorial coordination by Sabine Scholz
Production by Alwine Krebber
Color separation by Medien Team-Vreden, Germany

Bibliographic information published by Die Deutsche
Bibliothek. Die Deutsche Bibliothek lists this publica-
tion in the Deutsche Nationalbibliografie; detailed
bibliographic data is available in the Internet at
http://dnb.ddb.de

ISBN 3-8238-4579-9

Printed in Italy


**teNeues Publishing Group**
Kempen
Düsseldorf
London
Madrid
New York
Paris

Published by teNeues Publishing Group

teNeues Book Division
Kaistraße 18
40221 Düsseldorf
Germany
Phone: 00 49-(0) 2 11-99 45 97-0
Fax: 00 49-(0) 2 11-99 45 97-40
e-mail: books@teneues.de
Press department: arehn@teneues.de
Phone: 00 49-(0) 21 52-916-202

teNeues Publishing Company
16 West 22nd Street
New York, N.Y. 10010
USA
Phone: 001-212-627-9090
Fax: 001-212-627-9511

teNeues Publishing UK Ltd.
P.O. Box 402
West Byfleet
KT14 7ZF
Great Britain
Phone: 0044-1932-403509
Fax: 0044-1932-403514

teNeues France S.A.R.L.
4, rue de Valence
75005 Paris
France
Phone: 00 33-1 55 76 62 05
Fax: 00 33-1 55 76 64 19

www.teneues.com

**teNeues**